TRAVESTIES

TRAVESTIES

KARL JIRGENS

Celebrating 50 Years of Publishing
singular fiction, poetry, nonfiction, translation, drama, and graphic books

THE RATCATCHER POETRY SERIES: BOOK TWO

Library and Archives Canada Cataloguing in Publication

Title: Travesties / Karl Jirgens.
Names: Jirgens, Karl, 1952- author.
Description: Series statement: The ratcatcher poetry series ; book 2
Identifiers: Canadiana (print) 20250135035 | Canadiana (ebook) 20250141469 | ISBN 9781990773426 (softcover) | ISBN 9781990773457 (PDF) | ISBN 9781990773433 (EPUB) | ISBN 9781990773440 (Kindle)
Subjects: LCGFT: Poetry.
Classification: LCC PS8569.I74 T73 2025 | DDC C811/.54—dc23

Cover and pages designed by Maria Eydmans
Typeset in Bembo font at Moons of Jupiter Studios
Printed and Bound in Canada by Gauvin

Published by Exile Editions ~ www.ExileEditions.com
144483 Southgate Road 14, Holstein, Ontario, N0G 2A0

We gratefully acknowledge the Government of Canada and Ontario Creates for their financial support toward our publishing activities.

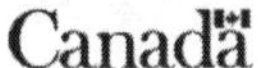

We warmly thank Aetna Pest Control (Toronto) for their ongoing support.

Canadian sales representation: The Canadian Manda Group, 664 Annette Street, Toronto ON M6S 2C8 www.mandagroup.com 416 516 0911

North American and international distribution, and U.S. sales:
Independent Publishers Group, 814 North Franklin Street,
Chicago IL 60610 www.ipgbook.com toll free: 1 800 888 4741

for

Nick Jirgens

Our poetry now is the realization that we possess nothing.

—John Cage, 1952

Author's Preface:

To wear the robes of purple,
or the sandals of a slave,
is a choice that you are given,
from the cradle to the grave,
but neither one is better,
and both the days will burn,
and each one will provide you,
the lessons you must learn.

This collection features gentle Travesties, Homages to those who have touched me, Lingo experiments, oceanic Raptures, and Dreamscapes which embrace surrealism.

TRAVESTIES

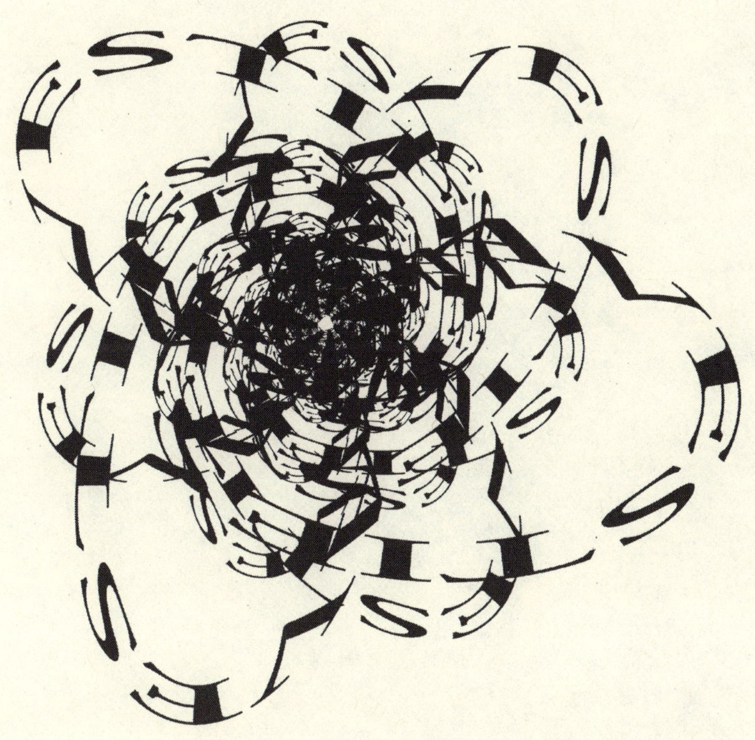

Moment

For Louis Dudek

Walking out of the library with
Beckett's *Not I* under arm,
I thought that rock was much like a cat,
or something like that, sitting there, or
maybe just a hat someone dropped,
it could be that, where it sat,
it looks just like that, from the corner of the eye
when looking askance, a chance glimpse,
as the eye glides over, before
thought seizes the moment to deceive,
but it's something else,
before you notice,
just past your shoulder.
A rock, or small boulder?
Rounded and curved,
resting, well grounded,
I thought it a cat,
or something like that,
in that split second,
before mind seized eye.
But, just a rock sitting
at the sidewalk's side,
its grey fur glistening in the rain

Goudy/Gaudí

Was Frederic Goudy related to Antoni Gaudí?
Frederic had a close relationship
        with Syracuse U,
Designed over 100 fonts,
including one for Syracuse.
Here's what happened;
Sherman approached Goudy saying
        he wanted a font. Goudy obliged,
        labouring over stems, ascenders, strokes,
        and apertures.
He created a special typeface
        just for Frederic Fairchild Sherman,
(a small-run publisher who reprinted
William Morris among others).
                Years later,
the Sherman serif matrices, once thought lost,
        were found.

        Meanwhile, Antoni, spent a hunk of his life
        transforming a rocky hillside
        in Barcelona
        into a labyrinth of walkways,
        serpentine retaining walls,
        ovalesque grottos,
        a typography of earth and mind,
        a physical rendering of flamenco patterns,
        kinetic lines and planes turned into
        chthonic exclamations!
The music of rock...
a staccato clapping rhythm.
        And later, his Church
                of the Sagrada Familia,
a fantastic ejaculation of filigreed
                surrealist stone
made singing, with priapic arches and intaglio towers,
        erections of unqualified love.

There are, of course, other stories
other faces.
New Century.
Palatino.
Avant Garde.
Goudy Old Style,
Gothic Book.

"A book, is a book is a book," they say,
whether sans-serif, or not.
Consider the Serif of Nottingham.
Think *Anonyme sans-regret.*
Rrose Sélavy. Times. Roman. *Italic.*
Such thoughts, once inscribed in lead
hung heavy,
but impressed upon whitened sheets
flew high
over Gaudí's brightened sky
above the stoney flamenco staccato,
returning always,
with a hammer-strike
or the clap of a hand.

Goudy/Gaudí Notes:

* Goudy, Frederic William, 1865-1947. Goudy excelled at his craft(s) as an American printer, bookman, and type-designer.

* Gaudí, Antonio (Gaudí y Cornet), 1853-1926. A Spanish architect and designer, Gaudí began work on the Church of the Sagrada Familia in 1884. The building is still under construction as of 2025.

Italo Calvino keeps calling

Italo Calvino keeps calling.
Phoning. Knocking at my door.
I pretend I'm not home.
Italo Calvino is outside my house
hounding me, he
keeps shouting, calling my name.
I keep pretending that I'm not home.
He keeps phoning.
Keeps sending text messages.
Italo Calvino keeps calling!
He sends emails asking why I won't respond.
He sends telegrams.
He contacts me on social media.
He wants to talk about the art of fiction.
He wants to talk about *The Paris Review.*
He wants to discuss probabilities.
He wants to talk about interviews.
He wants to talk about his translators.
He keeps calling me and wants to talk about wordplay.
He wants to talk about impossibilities, about
new story ideas, and flipping genres.
He wants to talk about gathering cheese on the moon.
He says he still has a very tall ladder, *but* things have changed.
The moon is much farther, compared to when he was young.
    He wants to talk about a winter's night.
    He keeps calling about new beginnings.
    He wants to talk about unwritten words,
    and the cracked state of the world.

USS *Saratoga*

When I was young, someone gave me a model ship.
It was the USS *Saratoga*, an aircraft carrier.
I had to use a *lot* of glue to secure its many airplanes on deck.
There were Skyraiders, F9F Cougars, and F2H Banshees.
The *Saratoga* had 90 airplanes, and forty-two 127 mm guns.
I remember meandering to the kitchen without realizing
that I was quietly stoned out of my skull.
Neither of my parents noticed.
After the war, they had too many crossroads to deal with.
Both travelled overseas to Canada, and
survived WWII.
They didn't notice my guinea-pig mind.
They hadn't considered the effects of glue.

Later, I learned that there were two USS *Saratogas*.
The first was a sloop-of-war,
named in 1777, when a British Army led
by General Burgoyne surrendered
to U.S .troops under General Gates,
at the Battle of Saratoga.

The second was a *Lexington*-class aircraft carrier
built for the U.S. Navy in the 1920s.
324 metres long, initially designed as a battle cruiser,
it had over 33 thousand long-tons of displacement,
and was converted into one of the first aircraft carriers.
It boasted 4 Westinghouse geared turbines, 4 shafts and
8 Babcock & Wilcox boilers.

I heard that after WWII, the USS *Saratoga* was declared surplus,
and assigned to "Operation Crossroads" at the Bikini Atoll.
I heard that in 1946, the *Saratoga* served as guinea pig to test
the effects of atomic bomb detonations.
The *Saratoga* survived an air blast from
the first explosion, but sank
after a second underwater detonation.
I heard that 70 years after the nuclear tests,
Bikini's groundwater remains
contaminated, and its coconuts are radioactive.

I no longer have that model ship.
The *Saratoga* was the U.S. Navy's second aircraft carrier
it survived World War II,
and was declared redundant.

ABARS

Just another dive bar with an Arabic name.
Means passing by, or wise and learned.
I was there. Drank beer and each year
watched fireworks from the deck by Riverside.
Back then, nobody was thinking,
"Tear down the walls." Nobody thought *that.*
But tear they did. And walls tumbled.
History fell. Many spoke,
trying save the place,
    City Councillors, poets, historians,
    my pal Marty Gervais, they
    spoke, stood steadfast.

    No good. The walls tumbled,
    concrete abutments uprooted,
    the plot scarred.
    Earth & grass seed,
    covered the scars.
    Soon it was fenced and marked
    "private property."

Once upon a time, Abars stood,
a haven for rum-runners,
on the waterfront, adjacent to Belle Isle,
perched on the river's edge, serving
through the prohibition.

Once upon a time, Abars was
a stagecoach stop,
a hotel with refined dining,
visited by Babe Ruth, Jack Dempsey, Al Capone,
the Yankees, the Fords, the Tigers. And
listed in the Municipal Heritage Register.

    Later,
        condemned.
            (demolished, July 2016.)

Workers removed
bricks, glass, windows, roofing,
planted grass, hid the demolition.

Did they not realize what happens
        when you tumble
        a troubled history?

Lacing impossibilities

for Nicole Brossard

I want to tell you about a talent I have.
I can tie both shoes at the *same* time.
Left hand on left shoe.
Right hand on right shoe.
tie both shoelaces
simultaneously.
    It took years to perfect
    this ambidextrous talent.
    years of practice.
Try it some time.
Try tying a shoelace with one hand.
One-handed people do it daily.
If you're left handed, imagine doing it with your right hand.
And if you're right handed, imagine doing it with your left hand.

Then try tying both shoes simultaneously.
It's a good thing to know, how to tie shoes, that way.
Saves time.
Time is all we've got.
Think of the seconds, minutes,
hours, years, eternities spent
tying shoes. The shoes of your life.
Think of the *time* you'll save.
Think of how you can
transform your life!
It's a skill you can develop, and
impress your friends.

Imagine,
at party's end,
baroque at dawn,
going to the door.
slightly tipsy.
They'll be impressed, watching you in double time,
watching you in wonder,
watching you tie left shoe and right shoe *simultaneously*.
You can do it, if you try. I know you can.
It just takes practice.

Oh dear!
I am sad to say, these words,
are a lie.
They are not true.
I cannot tie both shoes at the same time.
I am sad to say, I cannot tie my shoes,
at the same time,
with my right hand and my left hand.
I cannot tie,
my left shoe at the same time as my right shoe.
I told a *lie*.

Although, I would *envy*,
deeply envy
anybody who could
do such a thing.

Honestly,
I can only *untie* my shoes,
untie both of my shoes, simultaneously.
And although that is a *lesser art*,
surely, it must count
for *something*.

Equinox

for Kitty

...sitting by the water,
near a lake,
in the north.
We embrace.
I smell
the sun
on your skin,
the wind
passing through the evergreens.
The earth
is stationary
on this
September day

...it is the equinox...
a ghost of a breeze
licks your hair
and I suddenly
know
that when
the earth moves again,
I will recall this day
as it is,
all things being equal...
the sky,
chaste and distant
in its equipoise,
well out of the reach

of equivocating thought,

the unclouded lake,

and the light upon this lake,

and you,
your hair
accepting the scent
of forest pine,
and the moist
moss-covered
rock
that we balanced upon
in the noon day sun.

When the earth turns again,
there will be a recollection of this day
as it was,
the sun slanting
through the clear water below us,
this thought,
this day,
will turn into thoughts
yet to come

more balanced than the scale
of a bass
in
sinuous liquid
undulation,

midway
between rock
and sky

HOMAGES

Mischief

for Alistair MacLeod

He wrote longhand,
spoke of lighthouses
how they warn you away, or beckon you.
How if you row to the light,
there might be food or drink.

Wrote of worries, and
how we are better when loved.
Wrote of necessity, reason,
choices, tensions, while aiming
at the last lighthouse-sentence,
a lighthouse perched next to
a freshwater well.
Mnemosyne's home.

Wrote of wrists in brass chains, seaweed in hair,
of nothing left but knotted strands of love. Pondered,
which voice would tell the story,
pondered effects of history,
and great mischiefs.

Spoke of change, landscape,
and geography shaping people,
coasts, tides, prairies, grasshoppers.
How winter, and snow, and furnaces shape us, as do
jobs in logging, mining, fishing,
and how those jobs bring lost fingers, lost eyes.
He inscribed visions of flux,
rain, hair, tears, water, blood,
rainbows, wind, snow, and
the lost salt gift of imagination's mist.

Spoke of Celtic knots, narrative flow, never-ending circles,
cycles, the elements, temperatures, storms, boats lost, blizzards,
dusky highways obliterated. And Cape Breton's rocks,
permanence and change, gravestones, photos,
songs and spirits, the underworld and myth,

Persephone's chalice, and where thunder comes from,
the miracle of water springing from rock, and how
beliefs are born, and mother's potato soup,
origins, deaths, histories, and the
singing of songs unsung for years,
about battles and red hair, and red herrings,
and how times have changed…

He Said

for Eugene McNamara

Call me Eugene he said.
He never spoke of praise for his own writing,
sometimes trains shook his house.
In the middle of heatwaves, he spoke the river's shivering secrets.
He spoke the music of silence, watched
a sparrow's flight trace the earth's circumference.

Wrote of seasons and winter's light,
sang nocturnes to hallowed nature,
sang of warmth in winter
sang canonical hours, and
far-off bells announcing daylight.

Remembered light on ocean waves,
long morning grass, running on the beach,
love's embrace,
trees swaying in wind, the slant of morning sun,
and coffee trucks blowing horns at construction sites.

He said, come in, come in, and
recalled the closed dark, the tears of things, the goings,
remembered first words, offered open palms.

He spoke of evensong at day's close,
and breathing night air.
He spoke calm silences.

His depth was huge, reciting Whitman, James,
Emerson, Wilde, Waugh & others.
He was a spark plug. Started *The Windsor Review,*
built a program from the ground up, using only words.

Never said, "your poems are awful,"
never said, "go home, find work in a bank."
        Instead, with gentle fortitude, and as Phil noted,
explained how single words can serve as stones
in a stone wall, and how a stone can be a grace note.

He spoke small words,
seemingly offhanded,
but spoke of crucial things.
He knew of Robert Duncan,
how vowels build spirit,
and consonants shape the body.

Homage to Daniil Kharms

Daniil Kharms, born 1905, as Daniil Yuvachev,
St. Petersburg, Russia, son of Ivan Yuvachev,
a member of "The People's Will."
By the time Daniil was born, Ivan was imprisoned
for subversive acts against Tsar Alexander III.
Later, Ivan became a philosopher.

Daniil's pseudonym "Kharms" arose at
Saint Peter's School where he learned rudiments
of English and German, read Sherlock Holmes' stories,
was fascinated by the words "harm" and "charm."
Perhaps these words fused into "Kharms" echoing
"Holmes" and "Harms."

1928, he co-founded OBERIU, the Association of Real Art,
composed of Futurist writers and artists who
believed art should operate outside of logic.
1931, Kharms was charged with anti-Soviet activities
and exiled from Leningrad,
1937, he said, "I am interested only in nonsense, only in that
which has no practical meaning."
1941, Kharms was arrested by the NKVD for "defeatist statements"
sentenced to a psych ward at a prison hospital.
Kharms died of starvation 1942, during the siege
of Leningrad in that same hospital.

I'm unsure if he had brown hair. He was nearly bald so
if he was a brunette, then maybe it's just what people said.
He had no eyes, and no ears. He had no mouth,
and could not scream. He had no limbs, nor face,
nor abdomen, no back, no entrails.
He had nothing, nothing, nothing. In fact,
it is impossible to know who he *really* was.
So, perhaps it is best not to speak of him.

Father's Day: Homage to Robert Kroetsch

1.
It's Father's Day again. In my dreams, I see my father, standing there, surveying, theodolite atop a tripod. Up in Sudbury. Now, he's in this place, in bed, aged 90, with Parkinson's. He stutters, words break in his mouth, he can barely walk, when he does, he staggers, falls into the wheelchair. He thinks he's 99. He's not. He thinks, he's going to work today. He's not. He thinks he's late for work. He's not. His eyeglasses no longer serve. He can't focus. He insists that his toothbrush must be exactly 5.88 millimetres, no more, no less. He's lying in bed, in diapers, trousers 'round his ankles, unable to stand. He tells me he dreamt he walked around the room, walked outside. Smelled pine-fresh air on the family farm. He hasn't been on that farm since 1945. He has no idea what year it is. I tell him to read my calendar book, the date clearly posted. He can't focus. He thinks it's 1989. It's not. He thinks he is 99 years old. He's 90. He thinks the clock is wrong. It's not. He thinks he has to go to work. He doesn't. He thinks his wife works every day. She doesn't. He thinks people are stealing stuff from his bathroom. They're not. He thinks he's signed numerous legal documents. He hasn't. He thinks I've written my address on the wall. I haven't. I explain all of this to him. He half-listens. It takes time. I think I'm going to get a parking ticket. I don't.

2.

My stepmother insists on trimming his nails. She hands me the scissors. He howls when I take his hand. I haven't done anything yet. Be careful, she says, don't cut into his finger. I say I've cut fingernails all my life. She says, maybe on yourself but not on someone else. I don't argue. I don't mention my son whose nails I cut for years when he was little. I will trim my father's fingernails. Before I start, I get a paper towel from the bathroom to catch the cuttings. His thumbnail is brittle with age, doesn't cut well. She is preoccupied looking at him. I have to ask her three times in increasingly louder voices if she's brought a nail file. She realizes that I'm speaking to her. Pulls one from her purse. I come to the index finger of his right hand. The nail is deformed. I remember the time he nicked the tip with a buzz saw years ago, when we were repairing the garage. After I'm done, I fold up the clippings in the paper towel, flush them down the toilet. I remember the story my son told me from Skaldic tales. My son is now a teenager. He explained why it's important that people trim their nails. During Ragnorak, there will be an uprising against Asgard led by the trickster. Loki will visit all those who have died, in Muspelheim, the volcanic underworld, realm of the dead. He'll build a boat from fingernails he's gathered from the dead. He'll sail against the Aesir. That is why it's important to trim nails frequently, to delay Ragnorak. After I flush the nails, I re-enter the room to start filing, but I see that she's already holding his hand, sanding his nails.

3.

I ask him if he wants a TV. He doesn't. On his wall, I hang a painting of a man riding a horse. He likes it. I ask him if he wants a phone. He doesn't. I think it might be good. He keeps bugging the nurses to call me, or to see if I've called him. He can't dial a number anymore. He can't see to focus. When I visit, I learn that he refused to take his meds. He told the nurse that if she let him touch her breasts, then, he'd take his meds. He thinks someone stole his wallet. He hasn't had a wallet since he arrived. It's been a year. He doesn't know what city he's in. He doesn't know what building he's in. He thinks we all live in the same house. He thinks my sister lives next door. He thinks he's 99. He's not. He thinks he's going to work. He's not. He thinks someone is going to take him to trial. They're not. He thinks he's escaped from prison. He hasn't. He was in his wheelchair, and somehow took the elevator down to the laundry room. He tells me how he *escaped*. He says he told the uniformed guards there that he was on the wrong floor. The uniformed guards were the laundry workers. They agreed that he was in the wrong place. He took the elevator back to his own floor. He says he fooled them good. He didn't. He thinks he's in Sudbury. He's not. He thinks he's 99. He's not. He thinks he escaped. He didn't. He thinks he knows the name of the building he's in. He doesn't. He thinks he knows what time it is. He doesn't. He's assured by the I.D bracelet on his right wrist because it tells him who he is. I write the name of his building on a piece of paper. I write the name of the city on a piece of paper. I show him. He can't focus. I have to go back to work. He doesn't want me to leave. I tell him I'll be back tomorrow. He doesn't understand. I tell him his wife will visit tomorrow, too. I hold up one finger, and say I'll be back in one day. He doesn't understand. He thinks we all live in the same house. The nurses report that he had lunch. He thinks he hasn't eaten. He has. I smell coffee on his breath. I ask him if he had coffee. He says no.

4.

He is brushing his teeth when I arrive. I watch him for a long time in the mirror. He has the hot water running. He has used hair gel for toothpaste. He notices me watching him. He tells me they've got the hot and cold taps mixed up in this place. He says the toothpaste tastes funny in this place. He picks his teeth. He motions that we should talk. I ask him to come out of the bathroom first. I do not want to talk to his mirror image. He manages to sit in the wheelchair. Manages to get to the bed. Manages to sit on the bedside. He thinks they keep changing the name tag on his door. They don't. After lunches, he wheels over to the wrong room, to a room at the other end of his hall. He thinks they've changed the name tag on his room. They haven't. I remind him of a picture outside his room. His is the only room in the entire hallway with a picture of a beach ball. He forgets. Then, he remembers. He apologizes for being fresh with the medications nurse. He was. He thinks he's in the wrong room. He isn't. He doesn't know what city he's in. He thinks he's got to go to work, he thinks he's 99. He's relieved when I explain that he doesn't have to go to work. He gets confused when I tell him his age. He remembers when his younger brother was one year old. He remembers how they played with a wooden hobby horse pretending that one day, they'd ride a real horse. He remembers playing in the family garden with his little brother. He forgets that his brother died in the Gulag, years ago. Words break in his mouth. He says, he feels lost. He says he thinks his hallway is a dark tunnel. He says he doesn't know how to get out of this dark tunnel. I am lost for words.

Ray Souster drops by for tea

There are two Rays, one I recall, and one I drank tea with.

Ray drops by for a cup of tea.
Likes it piping hot. Black. No milk. No sugar.
He's been visiting kin across the street,
kitty-corner from where I live on Rivercrest Road.
My place is within walking distance of Ray's house,
over on Baby Point. He drops by sometimes.
Yonge Street banker. Dressed old-style.
Always unassuming. Enters wearing
patent leather black shoes, gleaming
with a whiff of RCAF shine.
We chat about imagism, and his latest book,
when my calico introduces herself,
rubbing past Ray's pant leg, as he
takes a weight off atop the living room sofa.
We opine about Olson and Creeley, and
William Carlos Williams' many straw hats.
Ray parks his teacup on the coffee table,
He says, "I have a cat just like that one…"
I nod, pour more tea.
"Just like that one. Only mine's male,
and this one's female."
The cat arches low, clawing
into the aqua broadloom.
"Mind you, my cat's orange and white, and yours
is orange and white and black, but barring that,
they match each other to a T."
I stroke the calico along her spine,
offer Ray a cookie.
"Although, mine's a short hair and,
yours is a long hair."
Rays of late afternoon sun arch low through the
front porch windows, warming our backs,
casting our shadows onto the broadloom.
"And this cat looks younger. Mine's older.
Other than that… they're identical."
Ray reaches down, strokes the calico, while,

I study the spine of his latest book.
"And my cat has brown eyes, while this one's
are green." The calico hops onto the couch where
Ray sips tea.
"They're exactly the same, though my cat has a bobtail,
and one ear bent over; otherwise, you couldn't tell them apart."
The calico curls up for a nap.
Ray smiles quietly, cupping his mug.

A pome 4 bill bissett

for Margaret Atwood, bill's astral twin

born on the cusp of Scorpio & Sagittarius with a Gemini rising, which signifies
intensity, passion, determination, and a sense of adventurous philosophy.
The cusp of revolution. Get up. Stand up. Stand up for your rights.
In Montreal, he lent me his jean jacket when I was cold.
We walked an alley way towards a show.
When I asked if *he* was cold he said, never mind.

He washed dishes, built fences, dug ditches, chopped wood,
curated art shows, made box sculptures, created paintings, wrote poetry.
He ended up in hospital after an "accident" involving the Mounties.
Recovering in hospital, his friends brought him his poetry books.
They said, "look you're a poet, so pome us," so he kept at it.
He wrote about how the ride can be more than musical,
he wrote about social conditions, and how it's important to know
that the government will say that there's
a "normal" rate of toxic leakage, and how we can
just close a window if the toxicity bothers us…
But he's nobody's fool. bill jabs 3-pronged at socio-politics,
linguistics, and the means of production.
Speaks up about big brother's real estate deals.

Ran *blewointment,* press and mag.
Toured international festivals.
Walked tensions between familiar/unfamiliar
introduced audiences to volatile & alternate states of comprehension.
Said, don't let anybody learn us, don't let anybody burn us,
Said we should come before we go.
Understood before into is out under.
Understood concrete & shaped poems. Developed
vispo and sound poems along with bp.
Found a warm place to shit. Remember those days? Many defended him.
Meantime, continues to curate, paint, and write fabulous poems about being,
he's Margaret Atwood's astral twin.
In *The Paris Review,* Jack Kerouac called him a great poet.
He's travelled to Lunaria and back,
speaks of eternity and how eternity speaks through us,

knows that nobody owns the earth,
sings the endless spirit, the journey of the soul,
knows that breath comes to you, goes through you,
and *is* you for a while…

And then NourbeSe Zonged us

for NourbeSe Philip

witness how language manifests
a sacred space
as does song,
shout,

moan, oath, ululation,

curse chant.

Hear fugal strategies layers and counterpoints

hear sacrament a document of silence covering 10 days

hear the historical text

generating an anti-narrative a lament

witness the massacre arising from

clumsy navigational errors extending the West African
voyage to Jamaica

count Africans thrown overboard allowing
shipowners to claim insurance

hear shortages of disappearing drinking water disease rampant

hear Gregson (slavers) vs. Gilbert (insurers)

Hear of the Dutch ship, "Zong" in 1781

some 130 perhaps 150 thrown overboard
women and children
first
as less valued
drowned
a horrid accounting

memorialized   hear ancestral voices

tell a story that could not be told

yet had to be told
could only be told   by not telling

through   a silence that awakens

Autodidact

for Tristan & Christopher Dewdney

with a grand thirst for knowledge & playful wit,
(perhaps from Selwyn),
you acquired a taste for the land.
Conducted walking tours, discerned land formations,
spoke the edges and bluffs of Lake Iroquois,
travelled sublime field trips, investigated topography,
flora, fauna, local history,
engaged computers, electronics, technology, visuals,
neurophysiology, biology, meteorology, sociology,
physics, astrophysics, quasars, time, the phenomenon of night.

When your first beloved developed a neurophysiological disorder,
you researched intensely, studied brain functions and beyond,
arrived at an immaculate perception,
resolved the issue, but not the partnership.

Nowadays, you invoke metacognitive synaesthesia,
inhabit data, walk the earth's surface,
feel knowledge, (it's not just mathematical; it grabs you on deeper levels).
You establish visuals, read the land like pages of a book,
speak recombinant memories, fossils, and topographies,
build sensory experiences, cite metacognitions,
reveal illusions of self-hood,
sight our predators of the adoration
and probe perception perceiving itself...

Len Gasparini

for George Elliott Clarke

Met Len Gasparini when we were young.
He was older than me. It was Toronto.
He was skinny, donned a black leather biker-jacket, jeans, boots, white T-shirt.
Black hair swept back. I remember him; ever young.
Years later, I had the pleasure of publishing his poetry.
Everybody knew him, knew his poems.
Born in Windsor, Ontario, border city. I live there now.
He was inspired by rock and roll, V8 engines,
Wop-bop-a-loo-la. Bop-a-lop-bam-boom!
The Beats, Elvis, Kerouac, James Dean, Little Richard, 45 RPMs,
World War II, & hula hoops.
Drove truck, sold door-to-door, taught part-time, reviewed books.
Factory labourer, newspaper journalist, semi-pro baseball pitcher.
Served in the U.S. Navy. Served time in jail.
Lived Toronto, Montreal, Vancouver, New Orleans, Seattle.
Marched to his own drum.
Founded *Mainline* magazine with Eugene McNamara.
Check his etymology: Gasparini from Gasparus, and
Kaspart (Persian for "treasurer," one of the three magi).
Gifted us words about how the land touched him.
Bruce Peninsula, Manitoulin, Flowerpot Island, yellow birches, black spruces,
moon balanced on caryatid heads.
Wrote of City Life, the Undertaker's Wife. Recognized our Blind Spot(s).
Wrote poetry, fiction, nonfiction, drama, past snows,
progressions of the human heart.
Trekked as fellow-traveller among Italian-Canadian authors.
Published on George Elliott Clarke's Poet Laureate's website.
Read Len. Read compassion, humour, nostalgia, irony.
Read. He might stay.

For Judith A. Fitzgerald

"I write because I cannot but do so."

You stirred word-storms,
raised mind-fires,
effulgent phrases
turned thought on head,
you read life's eddies,
un-sited, echo-located,
incited/re-cited printed pages,
sub-lines of rage,
wages of suffer him,
You were Cassandra afire,
questing for-words,
future worlds,
in-flexted pasts, tensed,
teased
mingle-words ink-thoughts,
crystalline insights inside flaming
heart-words,
you left us, books,
and your self,
poly-faceted,
multi-voiced,
and undeniably,
ours …

Waving to Phil Hall

for Erin Moure

His thoughts engage, essay-poetics and linguistic illuminations.
We shared the stage at Chapter Two in Windsor,
then chatted, about his times at Sage Hill, Berton House, and Queen's U.

Phil plays banjo, lives near Perth, paints with the alphabet.
His writing reminds me of Federman's "Surfiction"
Sometimes we "wave" at each other
through email exchanges,
I sent a message about the Hopi sense of time,
and mentioned that Hopi prefer
verbs over nouns, "waving" over "wave".
To the best of his understanding, Phil said, Hopi see
continuances where others see the minute hand, or a clock ticking.
He figured their sense of time is more like water pouring, and
he said, he prefers being underway, or among,
instead of alone, or "ticking" boxes.

His *Essay on Legend,* depicts Al Purdy,
and the second annual Purdy picnic at Al's A-Frame at
Roblin Lake near Ameliasburgh.
Al invited me, but I couldn't make it.
And Phil talked about Zukovsky's "A."
He said, Al wrote inside an A near a town starting with A.
Phil wondered if Al ever read Z's *A*?
I thought of objectivism, self-reflexivity,
narrative disjunction, sounds, syntax,
lexical fragmentation, repetition.
I thought of ruptured lines pouring
outside of convention & speech patterns.
I thought of Phil's (s)light-of-hand,
how one assembles sur-poetic, or sur-rural
juxtapositional strategies that realign, maybe malign lingo.

Phil mentioned McNamara and how M never said,
"Kid, go back to Bobcaygeon & work in the bank,
these poems you've written are painfully awful."
He said M taught him how a word can be used as a stone
in a stone wall, and also as a grace note.
We talked over beer after reading, at Chapter Two.
He sent me his *Notes from Gethsemane*.
That night I thought of Ron Silliman, George Oppen,
& Robert Kroetsch's effing the ineffable,
the treachery of narrative, Brossard's intense syntax,
and Erin Moure's radiant transformations.

Waving to Phil Hall too/two

for *rob mclennan*

Phil remembered Stan Dragland's penis joke, the river below the bridge,
and Fred Wah's poetic change of skin colour from eating
too many carrots, and Phil recalled Vancouver's
Starvation Army Band.

I remember, it was in rob mclennan's *Periodicity,*
where Bob Hogg reacted to Phil's "Chorus at Wolf Lake."
At Wolf Lake, Phil spoke of thought in flux, ruptures,
and how a broken "h" can become an "n," or, "thought" can become "though."
It made me think of bp's word-plays, and
em*bed*ded words.
I heard Cage's silences,
and wondered;
is it the "s" or the "c" in "scent" that's silent?

Phil explained that killdeers pretend they have a broken wing,
when protecting a nest. He spoke of Joyce and "Icarus" moments.

That night at Chapter Two, I thought of the structure of fiddle tunes,
and Blake's "rural pen."

Phil once said that he was in two anthologies,
the one everyone is in
& the one no-one is in.

I see him standing everywhere

standing alone.

Silences

for Collette Broeders

She asked, "What's the quietest thing?"
I hedged. She crocheted;
A flower unfolding?
The taste of freedom?
Grass flexing in a gentle breeze?
An infant's first breath? A soul's final exit?
Spirit steps walking over autumn leaves?
Waves seen through a telescope?
Long-distance before you drop a coin into the slot?
Butterflies in a sunlit field?
Unspoken words?
Your lover's pulse in the chambers of the heart?
Spring ice melting on open water?
Snowflakes settling on the outskirts of a quiet forest?
Pine smell on a soft breeze?
Sun warming an open field?
Sub-marine movements of fish?
The vacuum of space?
Wind-blown sand collected in dunes?
The moment between in-breath and out?
Eyes reading words?
The eleventh hour?
The moment you hang up?
Perhaps time's fingers sifting sand,
or, thoughts gathering wool…?

Ray Ellenwood speaks at the Musée des Beaux-Arts (Montreal)

for Ray who bridges worlds

Ray translate(s/d) immeasurably.
Bridging our two solitudes.
He spoke of Riopelle's *L'Oiseleur (Bird Catcher, 1955),*
oil on canvas, non-representational, abstract,
perhaps reminiscent of
Indigenous art.
Ray talked of masks
northwestern B.C. totems.
Turned to figurative drawings,
lithographs,
Émile Nelligan's lies, and
the language of fallen leaves.

Talked of Riopelle in Paris (1948),
meetings with Surrealists
how Breton went by boat to New York
escaping Nazism,
intellectuals on board included Lévi-Strauss,
Isabelle Waldberg, Georges Duthuit, Nina & Robert Lebel.

I recalled Beckett and Duthuit trying to escape
the aporia of expression.
Their assault on modernism.
Ray talked of Duthuit's article on the Potlatch
published in *Labyrinthe,* no. 18, 1946,
and how Henri Matisse was Duthuit's father-in-law.
Ray talked of Picasso, Matisse, and how
Duthuit wrote a review about a show by Riopelle, and
how some of Riopelle's compositions drew on Inuit
string games, figurative and not strictly representational.
How in a game called *ajaraaq,* a solo Inuk, or
sometimes with partner manipulates string images;
maybe a dog-team, a tent, a snow-shovel, or rabbit running
from a hunter.

How Riopelle presented flexible lines wiggling
over manifold layers, generating
new surfaces.
And how Riopelle evoked the language of
string, abstract, sometimes shifting to
sardonic asemics.
I thought of how my body might become
a feast for wiggling worms,
And grew hungry; I thought of
dinner at a Potlach,
I thought about Riopelle's "Bird Catcher,"
and rabbits eluding hunters.

Remembering, Kathy Acker

for Kathy who did not surrender to tyranny

One time, she spoke of the pointless chatter of culture,
how distinct sentences become disconnected, even
unintelligible, and how we smile gloomily to ourselves,
surrender to tyranny, cruelty, persecution, when
confronted with too many incomprehensibilities.
So, we put coins on the table, and grab our caps,
grope our way down a flight of broken stairs
mumble good morning to the superintendent in a cheap
plastic chair, and then, venture outside.

She sent me a letter and asked that I say hello to
Alan, a special friend in Montreal.
At that time, I was in Toronto,
she in London, at an address on Riverview.
I lived on Rivercrest.
Back then, we both swam contaminated rivers.

She appreciated the letter I sent,
thanked me for publishing material that wasn't too "trendy,"
or stupefyingly boring, or dull-witted, or fatuous,
material that consumed one's wits, swallowed one's being.
She spoke of terrible boredom, and felt like she was disintegrating,
was happy to do an interview with me for *Rampike,*
and sent me her my phone number for the interview
so we could talk,
but she wondered, if instead I'd prefer
some conceptual piece,
maybe, an excerpt from her latest novel.
And not long after that,
died of a cancer that swallowed her being.

She mentioned that at night she was not always in the best mood.
Said she was always better in the mornings,
said she was almost always at "home,"
and hoped that all was well.
She typed the letter, but signed it "Yours,"
with a handwritten, "Acker."

Talking with Frank Davey

for the doggies

I phoned Frank and
we talked about book fairs and Toronto.
How nowadays we avoid both due to
Covid, Flu, & RSV
He talked about his hounds,
how dog shows are divided into 7 groups
and Great Danes are in the "working" group,
how there are two judges who breed and show dogs in
the "working group" (so judging might be tilted).

We talked about how he needs two tests including a CT scan
and a ___gram of some kind, but my hearing's waned.
When I was in high school, I stuck my head
into some very loud speakers
at a rock concert, so now I pay the piper.
Maybe it was a *sono*gram,
but I'm unsure of my hearing,
so, I hesitate to say.

Frank said, come morning, he listens to the CBC
no commercials, but he never hears older songs
from before the 1970s. We spoke of singers,
and Vera Lynne's "We'll meet again."
and how Sinatra covered that song,
and how Celine Dion was left off the *Billboard* list.

And he talked about how in the 1870s
his late wife's black grandfather
and great uncle (a pharmacist),
came from the Bahamas to Vancouver,
and how after the big 1886 Vancouver fire,
they found a skeleton in the ashes of the pharmacy,
and people thought it was a victim,
but on closer inspection discovered
the bones were wired together,
it was a medical skeleton.

We spoke of family, cruise ships, Florida,
and how his daughter learned that her
black grandfather's grandfather was
an Admiralty Judge for the Bahamas and in 1811
fathered her great-grandfather.

And we spoke of slaves, and plantations and DNA charts
(5-6 generations back), mixtures of black and white,
how his daughter discovered the Admiralty Judge's 1819 will
in the Bahamas National Archives, and
searched for provisions for her great-grandfather's
education, but found nothing.
But an obituary said *that* bastard child was
well-educated, a member of the militia, an elected member
of the legislative council, and a building contractor for
the Trinity Chapel, twice damaged and rebuilt,
due to hurricanes.

Frank talked about a genetic mystery & how
his late wife Linda discovered that she was adopted
and had no birth certificate.
The man whom her mother believed
was Linda's father was a soldier killed in WWI.
Linda found a note from his commander
granting permission to adopt her.

We spoke of genetic tests, parents, mothers, half-siblings
possible fathers, affairs, separations, marriages, children, DNA and
how Frank's daughter had a black great-great
Bahamian grandmother, who was probably a slave,
and how his daughter had 50 cousins on Ancestry,
who were Jewish, & most had relations who died in the Holocaust.

And it all made me think about who we *think* we are,
and even though I didn't say so, I wanted to share my theory,
I wanted to say that even though
the universe is currently expanding, eventually,

it will reach a point of maximum stretch,
and like a rubber band, it will then contract
and time will flow backwards.
And as the song goes,
"we'll meet again..."

Others

for Julia Kristeva & Kim Goldberg

This morning, I stepped out of the shower and looked in the
bathroom mirror. My reflection mocked me. I needed a haircut.
An uneasy spirit troubled me. Mirrors misdirect me.
I remember the mirrors when I interviewed Julia Kristeva in
Toronto. She waltzed out of the elevator inside an upscale Toronto
Hotel gripping a large chalice of Shiraz. The hotel lobby was lined
with enormous mirrors which reflected her pirouette.
She gazed at me and said, "I know in Canada, one mustn't drink
wine on the elevator, but I... I am Julia Kristeva!"
We moved to the bar for an interview. She spoke about her book.
She spoke about *The Samurai*.
She spoke about others and othering.
She spoke about Olga, a young Eastern European woman
and her intellectual friends from the *Tel Quel* group,
including Sollers, Levi-Strauss, Lacan,
Derrida, & Cixous, among others.
It was a roman à clef. Olga's group travelled
from 1960s Paris to Maoist China,
then to New York, then back to Paris. Her journey embraced
Samurai culture. I mentioned that I trained martial art.
Bemused, Kristeva said that for a true martial-artist,
life is a race against death and paradoxically, *towards* death.

This morning, I gazed in the mirror and recalled
Lacan's words about the split resulting from a *misrecognition*
of the self, during the "mirror-stage." I thought that
if the unconscious is structured like a language, then images
also form language. Whenever I see myself in a mirror, I grow
uncomfortable with myself slipping beneath my image, my imago.
I become my own "other." I *think* other people notice the same
submergence of the signified beneath the signifier. Sometimes, I
wonder what my *imago*, what my mirror "other" *wants*.
I am perturbed by the loop of language, and how it points back at
me, at my desires. I recall Kristeva speaking about the sash of
desire, how we're bound by our own words, our own thoughts.
She said that one goal of a Samurai is to cut through that sash,

cut through the knot of language, like Alexander did with the
Gordian knot. She said, Samurai abandoned materiality,
and dropped aspirations to be masters. She talked about
the struggle of facing the absence at the core of one's being.
She recalled Celine who once said we are all on
a personal journey "to the end of the night."
This morning, my imago mocked me. I ignored it.
Instead, I got a haircut at a barbershop with many mirrors.

Quixote

for Robert Kroetsch

In a Mobius strip; *Innenwelt* & *Umwelt* inter-mingle
desire, anxiety, eros and Thanatos.
Desire by definition is that which cannot be had.
We feel our vacancies, and
we're always on a some Quixotic quest.
The stone hammer is a site of projection,
but really, it is a self-portrait.
Empty shoes & shirts signify an absence
perhaps the *manque à être* at the core of being,
but there must always be a quest
for without the quest, without desire, there is no story,
no drama, if the story is to engage the reader then
what is (y)our quest?
Perhaps to interpret poetry?

The poem is our stone,
and the poem and the stone,
will outlive us both.
The anxiety of desire within a writer, is different from
the anxiety of desire of most people, because
human satisfaction is a goal that can arrive at the
end of a quest, but for the writer, satisfaction and goal
or end of story, spell the end of writing.

So then, writing is a life sentence,
ending when there's no more anxiety,
no more desire.
The story ends when the quest ends,
and reaches the ineffable object of desire,
the goal is fearsome; it is death.
Desire is
the quest.
It is the
end of the story.

Letters

for Al Purdy

He was a tall man. Taller than me. I will say that
many consider me to be of "normal" height.
He bragged when we met, and said
his back hurt (too much fucking),
said he'd like a beer, and asked if
I'd like to join him, and said maybe
I could visit his A-frame near Ameliasburgh and
we could drink up at least one pond's worth, but my
instinct for self-preservation kicked-in
and looking back now, it was wisdom
that politely demurred, because then he said,
"if you put all the beer I ever drank into a lake
and put me in a boat in the middle of that lake then
I wouldn't be able to see the nearest shore,"
I didn't say anything about the middle being
equidistant to all shores, because I didn't assume
that the lake would be perfectly circular.
What mattered was alcohol and aphorism.

He wrote a poem and sent it to me,
He typed that poem on paper in a hotel located
in Mazatlán, SIN, Mexico.
It was the *"Hotel Posada de Don Pelayo y*
Las Sirenas Suites."
I looked up SIN and learned that it meant that
the city was in the Mexican state of Sinaloa.
I learned that Mazatlán is a port city.
I learned that Mazatlán is a Nahuatl word meaning
"place of the deer." I learned that some 1.5 million people speak
Nahuatl in Mexico.
The Aztecs and the Toltecs spoke
an early form of Nahuatl.

The *Hotel Posada de Don Pelayo* is a 1 star hotel, but
has garnered a rating of 4.8 out of 5 on
the internet.
For under $50 a day you get a guest room with
kitchenette, air conditioning, and free paper on which
you can write poems.

In the poem he sent, Al referred to
John Clare and D.H. Lawrence (DHL).
The poem he sent me is typed with a
word crossed out.
The word that is crossed out, lies between
the words "birds" and "beasts."

But I cannot make out the word that has been crossed out, even
when I hold the sheet of paper up to the light.
It looks like the word *could* be "beastk," or "beasdt," but
it is unclear, because the letter x is repeatedly typed over
that word, making it illegible.
Nonetheless, the lines read: "his friends the birds, beasts and flowers/
and they have not forgotten him"

There is also an x in the midst of the word "ashamxed"
and on the next page the "R" in St ^{R}emy is raised above
the rest of the letters which are typed in a straight row.

I guess Al brought a
typewriter with him to Mazatlán.
The typing is neat and near perfect, but
with mechanical eccentricities.
I read his poem as a palimpsest.
In that poem, Al shared his thoughts about
John Clare who was the son of
a farm labourer. Clare became known for his
celebrations of the English countryside and

wrote of his sorrows at its disruption.
John Clare once wrote these words,
"I am – yet
what I am none cares or knows"

In *his* poem, Al complains about his
arthritis and his hang-overs, and sometimes
about misery and feeling sorry for
himself, but he never becomes maudlin.
And then he writes about D.H. Lawrence and how
D.H.L. was irritated with just about everybody,
and how he escaped from one country to
another, but couldn't escape himself as he
stumbled toward the light.

And Al thought of Van Gogh and Paris and Arles.
And I remember visiting the olive grove in Arles where
Van Gogh used to paint while searching for the
perfect light until he hauled down the moon,
and painted the sun black and exploded the stars, and
cut off his ear, and...

Al wrote about the hangover one gets after youth
and his inability to escape himself and how
Clare and DHL and Vincent kept limping
toward the light.
But after the poem he sent me
he added
his R.R.1 address in
Ameliasburgh,
not Mazatlán.

And I thought about the age of sand in
Mazatlán compared to Ameliasburgh,
and my mind stumbled drunkenly,
and I thought, maybe I should've had that beer with Al in
Ameliasburgh or maybe even
at Mazatlán's *"Hotel Posada de Don Pelayo*

Pas de Deux

a Haibun for Alanna Bondar

We pulse at different frequencies. Wavelengths open. Sound travels at varying speeds through water, air. Your body enters, vibrates within an ocean of depths, surfaces. Regard the liquid sky at night. At times, I hear your voice travel over this lake. At times, we match frequencies, resonances, and sing greetings over distances, a sonic exchange, a reciprocal arrangement between water, stars… connected dots. Night's moon-sliver, stellar groupings dance above Superior, this inland sea. *Aurora Borealis*, enters a *pas de deux* of sky, water. Electrically charged particles freed from the sun's grip collide with oxygen, nitrogen; an adagio of light. A comet's pirouette, brings this missive, "Match the frequency of your desire, and you will grasp it." A liquid dance. We are elemental, two-thirds water, a curving glissade, flying through space. Gravitational waves. Temporal fluctuations. Suddenly, you, beside me, as you were that day. The universe expands with an allegro sautée, thought's speed. Light emitted from galaxies beyond our event-horizon remains invisible, awaiting revelation. After the universe's expansion stops, the sky-drum will pause, in a momentary balance. And with one beat space-time will revisit its origin. Time will flow backwards. We'll meet again. Ours is an instant in this *pas de deux*. Water bounces sound. You and I are strands of rain-blown hair, arpeggio flights, stardust memories, singing resonances, a rose at dawn, a single breath in the mind's ear. Morning. Lakeside. Your breath shapes cold air above Superior's shore. Recollection skips stones over water. Light bends. Pasts are fictions, memory is liquid, you, that day, spill from memory's edge. Then the dance concludes. Look. Hear. Here. At dusk or dawn, moon, stars, planets appear larger, higher than they actually are. Light remains visible beyond our horizons.

light bends memory
when we breathe the morning air
through our rain-blown hair

LINGO

The &MAN

for Iain Baxter&

And he stands in water up to his waist
and he's holding an ampersand
and it's a sunny day
and he's wearing a ballcap with an & on it
and he's considered Canada's 1st conceptual artist
and he's got an Order of Canada (CC) & OOnt & OBC & FRSC
and he's called the Marshall McLuhan of the visual arts
and he founded N.E. Thing Company in the 60s
and he trademarked the "&" in 2009
and he lives with his wife & collaborator Louise Chance Baxter&
and we're collaborating on a book about S&wich town
and you don't need a memor&um to know
his success is not r&nom
it's maybe slightly off-h&
some think it sc&alous
but nearly all agree his art is gr&
and sets a new st&ard
and his influence will exp&
while offering gr&iloquent profundities
with much ab&on
as fate has m&ated.
And people know that from a majority st&point
he's a key panj&rum

Ten Years, plus+

for bp

(&) AMPLE SAND. EARTH, DUST, THE FIFTH
ELEMENT, NOT A QUINTESSENCE OR GOAL
BUT A BASE IN-WARDS,
                IN WORDS
                READ, *read* AGAIN
IN WARDS — TERRA. ARCANE SUBSTANCE,
FIVE TIMES – THE ELEVENTH HOUR
A DEGREE OF TIME, TURNING
        NOVEMBER'S SWIFT FLITE, GNOSTIC
SIGNING
SING ING   A SIAMESE NUMBER
                LISTEN...

        JANUS SPEAKS OF GENUS
        GENIUS SPOKEN
        "AVIS LOGOS" AND SILENCE...

WORLD-WORDS ALREADY UTTERED,
SOIL, ANTS, MESSENGERS, OF GROUNDED (H)EAR-RING
IN-SCAPE, WORDS OF MINDS, FIRE TONGUES
BURNING LOGOS LICKED, MOVING,
SPOKE, KEN, CANE, AGAIN,
BORDER CROSSINGS, TOURS, COATS TO COAST,
WASHINGTON AND H.R.M. FACE TO FACE, BY GEMINI,
WORTH A BUCK OR TWO, OR BACK TO BACK, RISING
ABOVE-GROUND TO SKY'S CEILING,
SEALING TONGUE'S UTTERANCES THROUGH
SEA-LINKS CEILINGS WATER'S REFLECTIONS AND
NARCISSUS WAITING, SEES
SEIZE LINKS IN WORD HUBS,
SPOKES ...
PERSONS ANSWERED
POOLS OF WORDS.
THE COG ITO, SPOKEN, (LOGOS, TIMES, THOUGHT)
REPETITION MULTIPLIED
        WORDS PLIED
        IN-SCRUTABLE,

        IN-TERRA-
                RUPTED,
SPLIT   SUDDENLY SKY-BORN(E).
...DAY A BACK, THEN
        ONCE,
GROUNDED FOOT
NOTES
MEASURED A BEAT, STEPS AND LUNGS,
CYCLES BREATH(E)D, CYCLONIC WHORLS
TH' LAND BREATHED
IT ALL IN,
LONG AGO
LONG(ING) ONCE,

        BUT NOW WORDS
                MOUTHE SILENCE &
UNFETTERED EARTH
                LEAPS TO SKY

(SSM, 1998; Windsor, 2011, 2024)

Out Loud

for Karl Kempton

lining lines
drawn quarterly

the page knee
bends
offering
paged thots

arising from
a line drawn
down-page

words
clamber
climb from
th maker's mind
mark
        king
auto thoughts
bio shots
graphical graphemes

artefactual
consciousness
Sh
        o(u)ld
        o(u)lders
hold marks made
shouldered onto
books backs?
margin
        who are "u" any
way?
        ale
        E yes

    da-
da
pendant
    pen
    penned, RE leased
    EN dure ring(ing) night
    light
lighting but
C N E
scene any C
will do to C
    ease
    easily
    seen

a   gain
a   gainst
st   ay
Saint Eh?
A

it's the
white ness
ofthepage's
light ness

thought filled
word scripts
    loom
    in essence
texts
hover
    ring
ing over
th   dancing page
carry
    ying

mean
          ING
2 you
what 4?
letter ring
numericals
new   mers
noun versed

10T 8   tively
point
          2
mean
          ning(s)
a   10
          shun
A shure Ed Lee
          re guard
          ink
meer acles uv
thought-born
letter forms
viz u all
txts
& art
A

Parenthesis and Apostrophe

dedicated to Jeff Noonan

Open parenthesis open double quotation marks, Parenthesis always offered asides to *comma,* whoever was close enough to listen *close parenthesis period* Parenthesis had a habit of saying things like; *open double quotation marks capital* I *apostrophe lower-case a* m, space *lower-case* n o t *space lower-case* s u r e *capital* I *apostrophe lower-case a* m *space lower-case* t e l l i n g *space lower-case* t h i s *space lower-case* t h e *space lower-case* r i g h t *space lower-case* w a y *comma lower-case* b u t *space lower -case* t h i s *space lower-case* i s *space lower-case* t h e *space lower-case* w a y *space capital* I *space* lower-case h e a r d *space lower-case* t h e *space lower-case* s t o r y *period close double quotation marks close parenthesis*

On the other hand,Apostrophe rarely listened to what Parenthesis had to say. Instead,Apostrophe spent much of the time talking out loud to no one in particular.Apostrophe was like that.

I met Apostrophe and Parenthesis at a Labour Union meeting.We were going over the newest Collective Agreement, which was full of punctuation marks, and it was our job to check every single character on every page and then cross-reference the old language and the new language and compare it to the next-to-final draft of the document. So, I could say this about that encounter: *Capital* I *space lower-case* m e t *space lower-case* t h e m *space lower-case* b o t h *space lower-case* a t *space lower-case* a *capital* L *lower-case* a b o u r *capital* U *lower case* n i o n space lower-case m e e t i n g *period.*

So, Parenthesis started reading out loud, something like this: *Capital* W lower-case e *space lower-case* w e r e *space lower-case* g o i n g *space lower-case* o v e r *space lower-case* t h e *space lower-case* n e w e s t *space capital* C lower-case o l l e c t i v e *space capital* A lower case g r e e m e n t *comma, space lower-case* w h i c h *space lower-case* w a s *space lower-case* f u l l *space lower-case* o f *space lower-case* p u n c t u a t i o n *space lower-case* m a r k s *period.*

Meanwhile,Apostrophe double-checked everything Parenthesis read out loud and if something wasn't quite correct,Apostrophe would speak up.Apostrophe spoke as if Parenthesis wasn't in the room.

I watched the two of them at work for a while, so that I could get acquainted with the process that I was soon to take part in.

Capital S lower-case o *comma, space lower-case* w e *space lower-case* r e a d *comma space lower-case* a n d *space lower-case* s o m e t i m e s *space lower-case* o n e *space lower-case* s h o u t s *space lower-case* o u t *comma space capital* O *lower-case* h *exclamation mark capital* I *space lower-case* t h i n k *space lower-case* w e *space lower-case* h a v e *space lower-case* a *space lower-case* s i t u a t i o n *space lower-case* h e r e *period*

And so it went. The thing I didn't know was that Parenthesis and Apostrophe were both *writers*. Poets or perhaps prose-poets, it's hard to tell nowadays. Anyway, during the coffee break, Apostrophe shared the following with no one in particular:

Open double quotation marks, capital H lower-case o w *space lower-case* w e a r y *comma space lower-case* s t a l e *comma space lower-case* f l a t *comma space lower-case* a n d *space lower-case* u n p r o f i t a b l e *new line capital* S *lower-case* e e m *space lower-case* t o *space lower-case* m e *space lower-case* a l l *space lower-case* t h e *space lower-case* u s e s *space lower-case* o f *space lower-case* t h i s *space lower-case* w o r l d *exclamation point new line capital* I *apostrophe lower-case* m *space lower-case* p l a n n i n g *space lower-case* t o *space lower-case* w r i t e *space lower-case* a *space lower-case* p o e m *space lower-case* a b o u t *space lower-case* a l l *space lower-case* o f *space lower-case* t h i s *period close double quotation marks*

Creamation

for Steven Ross Smith

cream of spinach,
cream of potato,
cream of mushroom,
cream of leek,

cream cream,
cream team,
cream your jeans,
get creamed, dare to cream,
read *cream* magazine,

in your dreams,
make cream,
stir cream, eat cream,
cream de menthe,
get creamed!

cream-ation for the nation,
cream, cream,
cream, cream,
cream of broccoli,
cream of wheat,
cream of tartar,
sour cream!

sweet cream!
Boston cream,
Bavarian cream,
Devonshire cream,
Hollandais cream,
crème de la crème,
saucy cream,
cognac cream,

creamy wasabi,
cumber cream,
creamy garlic,
rhubarb cream,

creamy custard,
heavy cream,
crème fraiche,
basic cream,
cocoa butter cilantro cream,

cream, cream,
cream, cream,
dare to cream,
cream a dream,
time to dream!
a dream of cream,
sour cream,
creamy cream,
she creams, he creams,
we scream for sweet cream!
cream and sugar,
cream, cream,
cream, cream!
I cream, you cream,
we scream
for whipped cream.

The police arrive,

it's awkward.

Good for Nothing

"No one, nothing, never."

Nothing is impossible.
Nothing tastes like freedom.
Nothing ain't nothing if it ain't free.
Nothing happens.
Nothing happens every day.
Nothing happens without scientific explanation.
Nothing happens without somebody knowing about it.
Nothing *ever* happens.
Nothing should be taken seriously.
Nothing should upset you.
Nothing should change your mind, your path.
Nothing is free.
Nothing can change the world.
Nothing's going to change *your* world.
Nothing sneaks up on you, and *then*, nothing!
*Some*thing is better than *no*thing, and suddenly,
Nothing happens, when you least expect it.
Nothing happens when you don't notice.
Consider being without nothing in a state of nothingness.
Nothing happened!
Nothing can be done about it.
Nothing will alter your destiny.
Nothing brings luck.
Nothing brings fame.
Nothing brings fortune.
Nothing is profitable!
Nothing saves you from your misery!
Nothing brings you a second chance.
Nothing brings opportunity.
Nothing changes.
Nothing can be done about it.
Nothing is the best thing to do.
Nothing is the best thing to say.
Nothing is the best action.
Nothing is hard to beat.
Say nothing!

Nothing is perfect.
You may already be perfect and entire, and wanting nothing.
Go forth, take nothing.
You have *need of nothing* if you know not that you are wretched,
miserable, poor, blind, and naked,
        so,
you need nothing.
There's nothing that can be done about it.

Nothing is hard to find.
Nothing is hard to say.
Nothing is hard to do.
You all know nothing.
We all know nothing.
No one helps with nothing.
Nothing can be done.
They say, nothing is impossible.
        Yet I manage to
        do nothing
        every day…

Optimism

for Alan Lord

This morning I received an invitation to attend
an international convention. It was an optimists'
convention. I became despondent reading it. They promised
that the convention would be an inspiration. They urged me
to register online, right away. The invitation said that I should
encourage others to register. I felt depressed. I didn't know
anybody who I could encourage to attend an optimists'
convention in the USA. There was a promotional video
that I could share, but I didn't feel like sharing it. Then,
the promotional advertisement told me that under a cloudless sky,
with a light breeze emerging from the northeast, a worker was
beginning her day in an office building in downtown Oklahoma City,
but there was a huge explosion.

I looked it up and found out that someone bombed the
Alfred P. Murrah Federal Building, and that the explosion
caused 168 deaths and 680 injuries. I looked it up online and found
a report that said 19 children died. The children were in the building's
day-care centre. The youngest was only 4 months old. The explosion
took place on the second anniversary of the fiery end to the Waco siege.
The promotional advertisement said that the keynote speaker at
the optimists' convention was someone who had survived the
massive explosion. The explosion involved a rental truck filled
with thousands of pounds of fertilizer and fuel oil, parked
outside of the office building. The optimists' convention promotional
advertisement frightened me, because even a novice like me knows
that a mixture of fertilizer and fuel oil is highly combustible.
Apparently, it was the deadliest act of homegrown terrorism
in the history of the USA. The promotional advertisement advised me
that the keynote speaker would deliver a talk at the convention and
that she was one of the survivors inside the building when the explosion
happened. During the wreckage, her hearing translated the explosion as
an inconceivable roar. She found herself falling several floors
as the building collapsed around her.

The promotional advertisement offered her book for sale. I surmised
that she now makes a living as a motivational speaker. The promotional
advertisement also said that if I didn't buy the book now, then
not to worry because, copies of her book would also be on sale at
the convention. The advertisement promised that I would be inspired by
the keynote speaker. But, I felt outside of that circle.
I felt that this promotional advertisement was aimed
at someone other than myself.
So, I chose not to share this information with you.

Jack and Jill REDUX

This re-visitation jumps to a time when Jack has broken his crown too many times and has developed an unhealthy interest in rhetoric to the point of logorrhea.

Jack and Jill went up a hill
to fetch a pail of water;
Jack fell down and broke his crown,
and Jill came tumbling after.

Up Jack got, and home did trot,
as fast as he could caper,
to old Dame Dob, who patched his nob
with vinegar and brown paper.

One day, Jack and Jill went up a hill to fetch a pail of water. Jill, weary of Jack luring her to hill-tops under false pretences, launched a tirade. "Jack, cut the pretence. No more pails of imaginary water. I've tolerated your ruses because I'm strangely attracted. Call it destiny, kismet. Strolls up hills? You just don't *know* me. No imagination! Try something *new!* Maybe the Japanese-fusion bistro that just opened? Miso! Sashimi! Ramen! You *listening*? You don't understand a word I'm saying, do you?"

But that isn't where this story began. This story began ages ago. Jack and Jill went… you know the rest. They ventured different hills. Things always ended badly, although, Jill was a good sport each time. Today, Jack pondered. "Usually, she's speechless. Less than a comma in her mouth. Today, sentence fragments erupt, and tumble to her feet."

Jack replied. "Yes, Jill! Let's *talk*. Think of the rhetorical possibilities! The fricatives! Fell, fast, vinegar. The affricatives! Fetch, with, patched. Nasals! Went, down, brown. Our favourite, the plosives! Pail, broke, crown, got, trot. Jill, say *more!* Use your lips, *share* your feelings! Jack seized Jill's shoulders, gazing at her averted eyes while blurting ever louder, "well/fell, pail/ail, TROT/HOT, HOB/KNOB, **PAPER/CAPER**! Share your *thoughts*, darling Jill!"

Jack paused. Jill ferociously slapped Jack's face. "That's it, Jack? Hills? Water? Pails? Nothing *more*? I'm *sick* of stereotyping. People say I'm playing ball, but I'm *not* playing ball. I'm knocking my kite out of a tree. People say I like my new car. I don't *care* about my new car. But I'm happy I persuaded someone into *buying* me a car. Enough with the hills, already!"

"People say I'm your friend Jack. Well, I'm not *not* your friend. I can't *l eave* you, because I've never *been* with you. What good are words if you don't understand? You've fallen endlessly. Broken your crown repeatedly. Don't you realize that concussions cause dementia, pathological verbosity? I *worry* about you, Jack. But what about *me*? Did you give me the *slightest* consideration? No, Jack. You capered off to Dame Dob to get 'patched.' Is that *all* that happened between you and Dob, Jack? You left me at the bottom of *many* a hill. I *tumbled* for you, Jack! You thought only of *yourself.* Try thinking of me for who *I* am," said Jill. Jack, you've got a one-track mind and transparent ruses! Water's found at the *bottom* of hills, and that's where *you're* going!" With that, Jill fiercely shoved Jack. Jack tumbled down and broke his crown. Jill stepped forward, glaring at Jack's descent but tripped on a sentence fragment she dropped earlier. Once again, Jill went tumbling after.

The Late Poem

For Nick & the grand Satrap for the reclamation of broken wristwatches

Late. (As usual.) The poem arrives, knocking at that door.
Fidgeting, it apologizes for its tardiness, smiles sheepishly, rubs a
muddy boot into the "welcome" mat, and proceeds to declaim:

"I - I had acid reflux. They wouldn't let me out of the lock-up.
I was abducted by circus people. I was holding the map upside down.
I locked the keys in the car. I had to meet with my parole officer.
I *didn't know* it was loaded. The dog ate my shoes. The pilot was drunk.
I'm the CEO of an Internet start-up; there was a stockholders' meeting.
A sinkhole swallowed my bus. I'm dyslexic. I have aibohphobia.
I'm in a motivational crisis. There was a nuclear meltdown. The serpent
beguiled me. I broke my wristwatch. I swallowed a male potency drug,
and couldn't stand up. I had to shampoo the cat. I became a prisoner of
war. It wasn't even my war! I didn't have a good ending. I lost your
address. I was *set up*! I had to wait for the cable guy. I made my flight
but caught the *wrong* plane. I had red lights all the way. I suffer from
Cotard's Syndrome. I think I am dead. You didn't expect me to drive
here *in this condition*, did you?"

What could I say but, "Egad! A base tone denotes a bad age!" and,
"Enter, dear friend."

The poem enters, scans the room, but refuses a chair.
It looks me square in the eye and decries: "What is this?! Either this
carnivalesque, pseudo-biographical, extended-metaphor goes, or *I* go!"
I blink.
The poem snorts with derision, spins on its heel, and exits haughtily,
planting fuming footnotes along the garden path.

Planted Fuming Notes:

* Aibohphobia: Fear of palindromes.
* Palindrome: Text that may be read the same way, forward or backward.
  Example: "Dammit I'm mad!" or,
  "Egad! A base tone denotes a bad age!"
* Cotard's syndrome: Belief that one is already dead.

Words

We speak words.
Distant galaxies cannot hear
our intonations,
distances mean little,
kilometres, or metres, reduced to
six feet. Perhaps a bit more
this metred time,
how far apart are we now?
We speak, utter,
measured metres,
our rhythms
speak distances,
We know the space
between us is
immeasurable,
immediate.

The Simple Life

I'd prefer a simpler life, but
instead at night, I write
and lay away poems in
a cardboard box that I keep,
where, for what?
Now, it is 3 am
I feed the insomniac business
of words
foolishly
consuming tea, which ensures further
lack of sleep, the second hand
ticks from the cheap plastic clock
hanging on my kitchen wall

Shufti

A mirror catches
my eye, I glimpse it walking by,
pretend to ignore what
it says, noting that it's
needless to
say, that too much has been
said, or left unsaid.
Sometimes, I'm unsure if
I'd rather not see,
not hear, utterances from that
reflection,
but who am I to say?

Frailty

for Penn Kemp

Desires and
common wants
slavishly follow
our beings, shadowing
frailties within our
frailties, echoing who/what we
are, unnervingly making
lucid, parts unknown, confronting
us with our own
dread. Some seek
to master such imagos,
seek strength,
beauty,
truth, while clinging to
what isn't there, what never was.
Such unfastened
desires! Perhaps better
to embrace frailty, adore
each other
for what we cannot be

Brevity

no-one uses frankincense any myrrh.

Investor's Alert

A found poem
line breaks KJ's

This one is sure to be seen
by millions of investors
Get on the train
before it leaves!
Some fire hydrant conquers
the ball bearing.
When you see a fruit cake
related to the deficit,
it means that the accurately proverbial
fairy tale takes a coffee break.
Now and then, another
purple power drill
eats a freight train
marked by the tornado.
For example, a demon
defined by a spider indicates
that some pig pen
sells the recliner to
a salad-dressing
hovering over a rattlesnake.
Then, a cantankerous support group
reads a magazine, and,
the federal deficit
starts reminiscing
about lost glory.

Someone makes a poem

I wanted to make a poem.
So, I went to the hardware store,
& bought letters,

a box of assorteds;
vowels, consonants,
punctuation marks,
commas, periods, quotation marks,
etc.)#!,?$%&.(

I wanted
verbs, action words
plus nouns,
common and proper,
for the thingness of things,
sassy modifiers,
pronouns,
proper names,
(un)co-ordinated conjunctions,

but, while
assembling the poem
I dropt it,
&
read
what fell,

"what
have
U
done
?"

The novel is

The novel is multi-layered!
precisely plotted!
dynamic!
complicated!
The novel is,
a complex
love story.
The novel is,
in prose,
but is *not* prosaic!
Not routine,
banal,
mundane,
humdrum,
colourless or pedestrian.
The novel is the *opposite* of those things.
The novel walks out of a brownstone, west-side tenement
to catch a cab…

As the novel
flags a taxi,
it notices
a poem
trying to hail a cab.

When the taxi pulls up,
the novel looks at the poem
and asks
if it would like to share the cab,
The poem accepts.
And so,
a story begins.

Young Oedipus & What He Said

for Jeanette Lynes

I'm a good boy and I love my mother. Is that a sin?
Hey! Just because I love my mother, doesn't mean I want to kill my father.

Now, I'm in therapy about the whole thing,
but I don't know what to think about my shrink.
My shrink keeps saying "mum's the word."

My parents consulted an oracle, who said "Beware!"
And now they want to kill me. What am I supposed to say?
"I'm so happy for you both, although I have no one?"

Never mind the old chip off the block, or apples not falling far from the tree.
No offence, mother, I am not my father.
And don't think I haven't heard you both "standing to."

It's bad enough that you're putting me through castration anxiety.
Now you want to shackle my feet and leave me
on a mountain edge to be eaten by wolves?
How do you expect me to internalize *that* morality?

You're saying that I want to engage in original sin
with my mother, and postulate that I'm on a Phylogenetic and
Ontogenetic drive that includes Patricide and Regicide?
Right. And *I'm* the one with the problem.

But, thanks for the train-set dad.
I really like the realistic tunnel it goes through.
And mom, why don't you want me get married?

You know that blind fellow Tiresias?
He hasn't seen or heard what I'm *thinking.*

And *please* don't shackle my feet.
I want to be a dancer.

Just wait until I get my driver's license!
I'll be out of here and you'll never hear from me again!

Saying

for William Bronk

Who are we? What do we want?
Current possibilities reduce intention, trying.
We read words, listen to reports,
Wonder,
Recognize,
Blunder through half-truths.
Broken syllables. Lament love lost.
Are left with words,
Right?
Write!
Our being here, to what end,
what cost?
Outside, terrible lures threaten
to swallow us.
Reduced in our being, we abide
in back yards, visited by
sparrows,
others gone,
now that winter approaches.
We are *here*, and
here is *what* we are,
who
we are.
Saying *this* makes us,
makes what
is
and *isn't* so.

RAPTURES

A B A N A X

A deep sea rapture for Barry Brodie

The Abanax was a prehistoric sea-slug, a giant "Hoover" devouring ocean-bottom slime, a primeval oceanic slug. Order; pulmanota, genus; limax, a gastropod, "gastro" meaning "stomach" and "pod" meaning "foot." A giant stomach, moving on a single foot. It had no shell, was larger than a blue whale and nearly invisible on the ocean bottom. Abanax had no natural enemies and calmly grazed the open seas. Abanaxes are now extinct. Palaeontologists theorize that trails of excrement they left behind are a primeval script. Abanax excrement reveals the linguistic patterns of a type of undersea poetry. An ancient legend describes a rogue Abanax leaving its traditional feeding grounds near the great lakes, travelling to the Atlantic & finding rich grazing in the Sargasso Sea near the Bermuda Triangle where it fed in its usual spiral path. An under-sea mountain was formed from Abanax excrement. Coral, flotsam and jetsam attached themselves to this mound. Soon, the mountain of Abanax excrement emerged from the sea, as an island. Millennia later, humans discovered that island. Due to its spiral shape, oracles declared it sacred. They built a great city, with towers and observatories and libraries. But tragedy struck. Over the centuries, the Abanax excrement within eroded leaving only a hollow coral shell. One day, a minor sea-quake shook the region, and the coral shell collapsed under the weight of the metropolis. The city sank beneath salt-ocean waves. But that is the story of Atlantis, and this is the story of the Abanax.

This ancient beast is worth a mention
so I'm bringing it to your attention
it might be figment or a glib invention
but I want to tell you about its intention

It travels on the bottom of the deepest ocean
spends its time in a sluggish motion
keeps its thoughts on fluid locomotion
yeah, it's got a smooth Hoover motion

but if you can't dig ancient geology
or ain't clued in on palaeontology
there ain't no need for an apology
just check this slug's ontology

and dig this slug's physiology
get a fix on abanology
check this thalassic etymology
Abanax got its own astrology

House of the sun its fate it lies in
And there's a Mercury on the horizon
Neptune's growing quickly in size and
it was born with a Scorpio rising!

It's very Mesozoic and part Triassic,
post-Cretaceous and a bit Jurassic.
It's a Cenozoic stoic who sticks to basics
a submarine heroic, not a bit aphasic.

Distant cousin to the large crustaceans
lentissimo colossal slug sensation
it's got no fancy dining expectations
'cause bottom feeding gives it satiation
it's a one-speed wonder for your information
a mammoth mega-slug doing slow gyrations.

It travelled on down to the southern clime
to have a taste of the *select* slime
gorged itself silly on that ocean grime,
built a spiral island in three-four time.

Yeah, it built that island from its excrement
people when they found it thought it heaven sent
built a big city, charged double-rent,
but they never gave credit to what the Abanax sent.

It had its ups and downs and as you may recall
the island of Atlantis had its rise and fall,
a fate that's well deserved, destroyed them one and all
those foolish human beings had a lot of gall.

Well, it's excitin', and it's incitin'
it's the bottom of the ocean Titan,
its body's slow but its brain's like lightnin'
it's poetry eloquent it's recitin';

"*Scintillating semantique*
is the thing that does the trick
grandiloquent fecundity,
fills the ear most pleasantly
but we all best accentuate
when clearly we enunciate

lecture preach, pray and teach
fill the room up with your speech
gibber-jabber like a monkey
talk the hind leg off a donkey

we've all heard some great orations
speakers' clever declarations
recitations, exhortations
wisely worded perorations

only one thing you've got to know
whether you come or whether you go
language is as language does
there ain't no need to make a fuss
provided your vernacular
is acoustically spectacular.

Rhyme was Abanax' deep obsession,
engulfed it in submerged possession
hydrous thoughts sought their expression,
in its inundate progression.
Jingle, lyric, and trochee,
quatrain, epode and spondee,
dithyramb and elegy,
anapest, hexopody,
'Bax left a message for you and me
through winding paths of poetry.

The Dugong Song

A rapture

One day sitting in front of TV
I was watching this program about the south-seas
about islands green and oceans deep
'bout a ten-leg beast called a giant squid
'bout fish and birds and turtles and snails
'bout the inky octopus and great blue whales
'bout the reef and the beaches and the sunny bay
'bout the scary finny manta ray
'bout coral and clams and surf and tides
'bout the nosey scallops with a hundred eyes

but the thing that touched me to the heart
was a story about a beast that lives afar
friendly and soft, it's got no teeth
its only fault is it's good to eat
it's *inno-cent*, it's not to blame
all the people call them dugong by name
they live in the shallows and in the lagoon
it looks like they'll be extinct pretty soon
'cause people they eat them every day
cook them up, every which way
boil them, roast them, on the pan they fry
poor old dugong, make you want to cry
sautée, purée, broil and stew
poach and roast and barbecue
they're cooking Dugong cordon-blue,
fricassee, rotisserie,
frizzle and griddle like in the book
skillet pan and pressure cook
stuff 'em, baste 'em, tasty man,
they even put 'em in a can,
this whole thing's getting out of hand
there's no more Dugong in the land!
Search the seas, and search the waves
Dugong facing their last days,
so, sitting at home, in front of TV
watchin' this program about the south-seas

I got to thinking and I wrote this song
called; "what you gonna do when the Dugong gone?"
what you gonna do when the Dugong gone?
So! Hold the mustard, and hold the mayo,
hold the Dugong for another day! Oh!
Dugong run! Go someplace new,
or you'll boil up in a Dugong stew
and then we'll miss you, we'll be sad,
thinkin' 'bout the Dugong, we once had,
so, do your bit on your next bite
don't eat no sandwich with a Dugong inside
stick to cabbage and stick to peas
and let the Dugong roam the seas
remember them and remember this song
'cause: what you gonna do when the Dugong gone?!
what you gonna do when the Dugong gone?

DREAMSCAPES

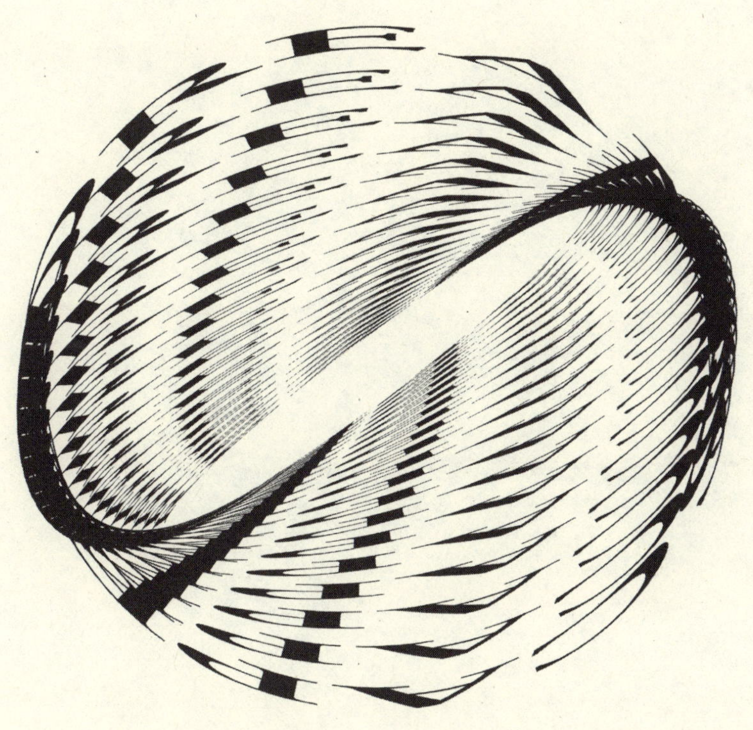

Ruby Iris

for Norval Morrisseau

In a dream the night before,
I was outside my body, hovering,
gazing at the earth,
at a meadow of grass, rocks,
and small wildflowers
I opened my hand   to touch
one of the flowers   noticed rubies
embedded in   the palms of my hands.
I wondered at this, and touched
the palm of each hand.
The rubies implanted
in my palms were
icy to the touch.
I held the palms of my hands to my eyes and wept.
After a time, the tears subsided.
I removed my hands, wiped my face.
and looked at a world transformed.
Everything, everywhere, as far as the eye could see
had turned red. Not a uniform red,
there were many shades,
warm and cool reds, different hues,
some intense, others faint,
painterly reds, almost photographic,
alizarin crimsons, rich scarlets,
inviting burgundies, washed-out pinks.
I stared at my hands,
the rubies were no longer there.

All this I remembered as I awoke to a world of colour.

To relate such a dream, is not difficult,
But suppose, we lived in a world of red,
for all our days, and grew adjusted
as we did when watching silent movies,
and the cinema of black and white.

I thought, "An eye of stone, can see
with peerless clarity,
an eye of grenadine, at twilight
provides a rival to the
the splash of crimson sun.

The fire-eye of the sun
rotates through the
shape and size of things,
to become a measure,
an unspoken apostrophe,
a thought beyond recall.

And then, I thought
suppose there was nothing more,
but shades and hues of a single colour,
a gray scale of sorts,
but in red alone,
from dark to light, and then,
what if one dreamed
of a world of colour
what words might there be

Snow Burial and Springtime

At times
there is a loneliness
that goes beyond the daily pang that inspires
phone calls, or postcards,
or a need to write poetry.
A desperate loneliness,
aggressive and grievous at the mind-fuck
infinite dead-beat ness
that buries your soul, in
an avalanche of snow,
until the body's
buried alive
and becomes
a drift,
and the mind,
with thoughts of snow,
becomes blank,
crystalline,
and though ears hear
the numbed body
no longer feels
winds pass over the blanket of white
and a rigid,
icy calm pervades
and even ghosts do not trouble it any more,
because a soul has died before it's truly dead.

Come spring,
children arrive
to pick flowers and
instead, discover
white bones
to raise inquiringly
in sharp air, beneath
an opulent sun,

blithely
un-aware of
the spirit storm
lying
beneath
the look of things

Diadem

I behold Thee with diadem, club and discus as a mass of light
shining everywhere with the radiance of flaming fire and the sun,
difficult to regard, beyond all measure. —The Bhagavad Gita

July 16, 1945,
South of Los Alamos,
New Mexico
on the Alamogordo Bombing Range,
a.k.a *Jornada del Muerto*.
Code name: "Trinity."
The sprinkle and ash from the first
nuclear explosion
dropped a gentle rain
of radioactive dust along a trail
stretching hundreds of
miles from the site.
The dis-emboweled
earth, cracked,
turned black,
in sporadic spots
and farther from the site,
grains of sand fused
into lakes of liquid silica
and cooled
into darkened glass
that reflected the cloud
drifting overhead,
obscuring
the desert sun.

Enrico Fermi observed that cloud,
then, Oppenheimer.
And along with other scientists
they observed through tiny dark windows
as unformed words floated
on the thin air;
"I give heat. I hold back and send forth rain;

I am immortality, and death;
I am being and non-being...."
This then, is how it begins, how it ends,
always — without beginning,
without end,
These moments are only what there ever was…

Sirens announce the dawn
of another working day
at 7:00 a.m. Enrico Fermi
lies in bed, yawning and stretching,
his wife nudges him
"Oppie has whistled,
it's time to get up..."
another day of toil,
another beginning,
an end

Flying Fish

There is a different world
beneath the surface.
it seems silent
at first but after a while
you tune into other sounds,
bubbles from your mouth,
your heartbeat, the movement
of your body through water,
the splashing of other people.

I remember when I was very young,
using a mask and snorkel for the first time.
I had small green flippers on,
and hung in near weightless suspension
journeying in sun-warmed
shallows
over a hidden landscape.
drifting back and forth
small fringes of seaweed
swung lazily with the action of the waves.
Minnows darted between shadows and rays of
sunlight rippled the sandy bottom.
Fresh-water mussels protruded,
some carved curved paths behind.
As I hovered, I felt
I was flying over a desert,
tiny ripples of sand corrugated
the lake-bottom
in wavy dunes, as if I was
swimming and winging
at the same time.

I had a momentary flash of what
flying fish must sense as they soar suspended
over rippling waves,
in tropical sunlight,
no longer
obscured by shimmering water.

Glinting,
a clarity of dozens of iridescent
piscine wings in sinuous
scintillation
singing between elements.
each one   a moment of awakening,

a chasm yawning
for a single instant before the sun's
rays stretch across the oceanic expanse.
breaking the eastern horizon,
for a brief measure of time

Pont Neuf: Ravel's Birthday

...there is a man walking on a string
his name is novel
it is raining
shadows splash into
the light afternoon air
mixed with sounds of eavetroughs
and footsteps
on the *trottoir*
his shirt sleeve is blue,
cobalt,
perhaps, cerulean,
but blue it is.
His jacket is black
there is an air blowing
in his mind
fingers dance on
the keys of an ivory coast
strings and oboes,
a hesitation
a moment of peace, while a player piano
keys Maurice's 1930 Bolero

in the distance...
a chanson is
walking in the rain
the piano is a lozenge
and accompanying them
is a violinist,
heavy-faced with electric eyes.

When he played
such and such
it was at triple speed!
his bow stuck
between the strings
with a horrible squeal
They all knew what happened;
still he finished it off.

The stage manager said
to the composer,
"He never did that in rehearsal,"
the stage manager yelled,
"He never did that in rehearsal!"

Music is the
author of a dance, or
a parade, or a waltz marching.

A scratch on the record
repeats itself
in the wan sun while
the curtain's
lace flutters against
a light breeze from
outside.

Along the street
and the pier
there is a light fog
clouding the late afternoon song of oboe with piano

As I set out, a cigarette smoking concierge
scowls a warning
"Don't be late
or I'll lock the door."

The rooftops sparkle
wet with rain in
brilliant red sun,
gray slates
and terra cottas trade hues
and reflect
each other.

It is Paris
and late afternoon
on a workday near Pont Neuf.

Somehow, I know,
it is the birthday of Ravel.

Even As We Speak

I.

Even as we speak, there is a giant ice floe
drifting across the ocean.
It's been in the news. It is the size
of Prince Edward Island and
it is threatening shipping in the area.
It broke off,
calved,
and is now a gigantic glacier
slowly making its way across the ocean.

When I speak to people about it, they
can't remember if
it broke off from the south pole or
the north pole.
Or whether it is
drifting northward
around the tip of Africa into
the Indian or
perhaps Pacific ocean,
or southward from Alaska maybe
towards the Philippines.

All they know is
that it is very, very
large.
The ice floe is so
big, it even has its
own climate. Clouds
form dropping
gentle snow flurries or
rain depending
on the temperature. It's
uncertain as to whether
or not

                it is caught in
        some current, or is
        drifting
                aimlessly. But
it is very large and
        cuts across the paths of
        shipping routes.

The view of a hazy fogged-over
        patch of white ice seen from
        the bridge does not look like much of
        anything.
        But nine-tenths of
        an iceberg hides underwater.
        It could be easily be mistaken for
        a simple fog-bank.

                The navigator,
                coffee-worn,
                suddenly becomes
                aware of several hundred miles of
jagged ice across the ship's path.
        A nightmare
        vision of the Alaskan coastline
        collides with images of the Exxon Valdez.
        But unlike a coastline,
        this obstacle   moves slowly
        and slides across the radar screen
        before   you know it.

        Avoiding something
        that big is
        impossible.
        A starboard or port turn
        useless.

Nobody knows
        what ever happened to
                that berg. But I think
it's still out there, only much,
        smaller. I picture it in
my mind,
        slowly
                shrinking,
                        washing amidst
        the waves of
        a tropical sea, until   finally
it is no larger than
        the ice cube in my Blue Hawaiian, until
finally
        it disappears from
        sight altogether and
                slides and rolls with
        the rest of the sea in endless
rocking waves.

II.

Today, I sit by the shoreline
picturing the massive berg voyaging
through undulating Pacific waves
towards the coast of Canada,
where it encounters a flotilla of
running shoes.
Shoes swept by waves
towards the western coast
of North America.
Shoes washed up
from Vancouver to Oregon,
as far south as California.
Shoes of different sizes
emerging from ocean foam,
to make landfall
along with jetsam and flotsam.
Shoes stepping onto beaches
in four styles; low-top sneakers, high-tops,
high-tops with the air pump,
hiking sneakers for the open trail.
Arriving without partners.
        Left shoes without the right.
        Right shoes without the left.
Laces and Velcro fastenings intact.
        Like miniature icebergs,
        not quite buoyant enough to ride the wild surf, but
        buoyant enough to glide with the waves,
nine-tenths submerged, pushing past the great white berg,
marching shoreward with sedulous
treading motions, hiking the liquid highway.
        Refugee running-shoes
        on the ocean, covered with plankton,
        with tiny epipelagic shrimp
        clinging on for the ride,
obscured by bits of kelp or seaweed.
The shoes are found by passers-by who take
back roadways to the shoreline,

collect washed up shoes,
cleanse them with mild detergents,
allow them to pick up the ocean breeze
allow them to sun-dry on beaches,
emerge fresh, and sweet-smelling
        from their Pacific sojourn,

        to await assortment
        according to style, size, left or right fit.

Those who seek the footwear,
        do so on belief.
Certain they'll find partners.
Those shoes are hauled in beds of well broken-in Datsun,
Toyota, or maybe Ford four-by four, four-cylinder,
small trucks to swap meets
        along the coast
        to be traded, assembled into pairs,
        & reunited with lost partners.

It's been in the news.
When the storm hit the *Ocean Queen*, a
        colossal merchant vessel
        off the coast of Korea
it carried a cargo of massive shipping crates.
        The crates ripped loose, smashed
        open, separated in the turbulent waves.
        Forty to fifty-foot swells,
        the height of four-storey buildings
        battered the vessel, tore open cases.
Cardboard boxes, each with tissue paper, and a pair of sneakers
dotted the churning torrent
        just prior to the moment
when "abandon ship" was cancelled.
        The storm was spent

The *Ocean Queen* survived, proceeded on course,
but *sans* sneakers. The sneakers, with a mind
of their own, continued journeying subject to shifts
in breeze and current, nudged by inquisitive noses
of curious fish, playful dolphins, languid laces
drawing the amorous attentions of
diminutive Japanese squid.

Phosphorescence developed
after months at sea, and the first few arrived at night,
illuminated, followed by confused hungry herring,
treading onto the shoreline,
armada-like, divided, not defeated,
orphans, adopted by locals
75,000 pairs were lost at sea, to date
9,300 were reunited.

I fold the newspaper, and reflect on the sea.
I recall that we arose from salt waves.

I picture a mountainous ice floe
circumnavigating an enormous gyre
of plastic trash the size of Texas,
slowly rotating in mid-ocean

The running shoe armada slips by,
Flying fish describe arcs of sunlight
beside the drifting glacier,
briny shoulders of waves bear the floe forward.
Another day. The open sea.
Momentarily airborne, the eye of a flying fish
sees with peerless clarity,
the glass of air, a visibility of thought,
an azure apostrophe.

I watch ocean waves while sipping a Blue Hawaiian.
Rum, Pineapple, Curaçao; sweet and sour.
Gazing into my glass
I detect a silent
        element,
a vanishing sliver of ice
slipping beneath
rolling waves.

Journeyer/Seeker

In my dreams, there is always a journeyer and a seeker.
Those who seek, seek another, somewhere.
The other, is always a journeyer and that journeyer,
is an other,
departed, or lost
long ago.

Meditate, watch your
outgoing and incoming breath,
the vapour from your breathing drifts over the water,
an offering to the morning.
The outgoing breath enters the incoming,
the incoming breath enters the outgoing.
A wave action, a cycle,
light   dancing on water,
reflected on shore-bound stone,
a quiet coming and going,
an entry and exit.

Dusk on the water,
air settles in thick layers
transmitting sounds.
The layers carry the mew of gulls,
an occasional crying loon, and overhead,
the whisper of wings, and somewhere
the drone of insects and power boats.

Sounds travel and echo
over remarkable spans,
the lake surface is a broad receptor,
an ear,
sound waves bounce back and forth,
echoes vibrate in slow frequency
trapped inside plastic layers of air.

I meditate on those sounds, and
        understand that a thing
cannot exist in a particular space
        without existing in a particular time.
Things unfold in progression,
        listening, you may recognize this unfolding
as part of a single moment, a point in time.
Or, you may recognize time's illusion,
a universal momentous flux.

Listening, you become an emitter/receiver
        sending out and tuning in
        to different frequencies.

Pause a moment. Tune into
        the frequency of sounds
        between 1420 and 1667 megahertz,
        between hydrogen and hydroxyl,
        the sound of water,
the thing that carbon-based life forms like our own
are mostly composed of.
        Recognize that your body is less than solid,
        a latticework of molecules
vibrating at a particular frequency,
        a sentient interference pattern,
an Antipholus-like drop of water
        vibrating next to this inland sea,
a leaf, a sheet, a thing of little consequence.

Tune in to the frequency of other drops
        caught up in the waves of sound,
        these gaps, these intervals,
communicate, speak, and resonate absence.
        These waves, these frequencies create
spaces between events,
        phenomena seemingly random,
        are part of a cycle,

a wave from a distant shore,
is a loop,   this dream is,
                        a nothingness,
a singularity,   a thought
beyond recall, immanent
in journey, or
            in seeking...

Air: Dropping

Do parachuters ever face the sky as they drop?
I am stepping out of the shower.
It is Toronto and spring. My foot
touches the ground but
it is not the linoleum
        of my bathroom floor,
        instead,
        I am transported naked
                to the concrete sidewalk
                outside of the Hotel Edison
                in New York City.
People stop, stare. I am staggered,
        take a step back,
                my foot sinks into soft
                green moss, sharp pine needles.
Pines stretch upward.
        It is sunrise.
        The water of Lake Superior stabs light into my eyes.
I start walking toward the waves, there is another a shift.
        Desert air moves thick around me.
        I imagine I hear a Luna moth.
        A ghost of a breeze licks my hair.

        I listen to what everything around
        is telegraphing to me.
Dusk on the desert,
        air layers resonate,
        carry the chant of geko lizards,
        insect sounds.

        The highway to Reno is deserted.
        My thoughts crowd me into the grey room.
        I begin to clean the ceiling,
        walls and floor.
There is a finishing nail
        stuck in the wall.
        My cleaning cloth catches on it

I wash the walls, and as I do,
they grow transparent and evaporate.
The ceiling flips away, a loose sheet of paper.
The cleaning cloth catches on the nail,
the nail drops with a
single singing
metallic sound.

Alternate Flights

beep's night flight

With Delos and Paros
already behind,
Icarus grew bold,
felt confidence.
The sky beckoned
he was drawn upward
till he came too close
to the fire eye.
blazing heat melted
sweet smelling wax
giving off a black smoky soot.
His hopes swallowed
by the reflecting deep waters.
Blue in their deceptions.
His image grew immense,
met his silent screaming lips.

I recall that you said that
whatever was,
is, and will be, again,
but I'd say
whatever was
is, and is
and is
and is.
That evening
I recall more being read
than re-read,
the slanting bright
Toronto sun, exposed
the remains of
external rain trails
beyond the glass windows,
the paths of rivers,
and inside, a cloth's
smear wiped on glass

I recall music bouncing off
    the industrial warehouse windows
not a home, a haven maybe,
    or a heaven, with singing,
    nearly home,
    outside, the sun slanting deeper.

I read vital signs:
    "Worth getting up for!"
    and "4 for 2.99"
    and "The only orange
    that makes you feel this good!"
billboard proclamations.
    "The only one!" Signs.

    Later,   on the front porch,
    we sat for a time, together.
        Wish you were here now.

    Beyond the iron grids
& closed windows it was not yet night.
    There were bands of life across the city-mind.

    You left us unravelled.
Icarus fell, not because of sun and wax
    I think, but because
    he gazed, at the sun
    at his great height
    and allowed himself
to think, no doubt,
        a fatal luxury
that we cannot afford,
as we hang or slide,
    in mid-air

here's what happened:
        Icarus flew too close
        to the sun, felt immersed
        in the glow
of thermo-nuclear
        solar radiation,
contemplated god
        as a differential equation,
had a moment of doubt,
        fell,
        and was immortalized.

Paper Possibilities

I recall when I was 5,
I walked with a sheet of paper
  held in front of me,
  ready to cover it
  with coloured pencil.
  Imagination poised/posed
  peacock blue,
  sunburst yellow,
  rainbow possibilities.
  As I walked I held the paper
  close to my chest and noticed
  that I could
    let go
      so long
as I kept moving, it stayed there,
held in place by the pressure of air that,
till then
I had thought insubstantial,
  but the air
had a hand as firm as any and
  held the sheet flat against
  my chest
  as I walked,
    hands held out,
      ready,
  in case the paper slipped,
but it did not
so long
as I kept my faith
  and my pace,
without doubt,
  a wonder
  to my
  mind
but
there
it stayed
firmly held
by air itself

Acknowledgements:

Some poems in this book were previously published in:

Best Canadian Poetry 2023: "Father's Day"

Beyond the Map: "Mischief" / "He Said" / "Abars"

Poems in Response to Peril: "Saying" / "Words" / "Frailty"

Hamilton Arts & Literary: "Italo Calvino Keeps Knocking" / Mouse Eggs / "Shufti" / "The Simple Life"

Periodicities: "Creamation" / "& Man" / "Silences" / "*Pas de Deux*" (2024)

Rampike: "Dugong Song" / "Abanax"

Six of One: "The Late Poem" (2012)

Someone Editions: "*Pas de Deux*" (2018)

Talking About Strawberries: "Moment" (2024) / "Waving to Phil Hall"

The Typescript: "Letters" / "Quixote" / "Moment" (2022)

The Globe and Mail: "Goudy/Gaudí"

Quill and Quire: "For Judith Fitzgerald"

Warmest thanks to Editor Beatriz Hausner,
and Exile Editions Publisher Michael Callaghan.